ENDORSEMENTS

In God's sovereignty He raises up unique people for unique tasks. I feel that He has done this with Ron DiCianni. I've met few people who have both the passion and the ability to do what Ron does.

Max Lucado
Best-selling Author

"Artists 'feel' things deeply—I should know, I am one. And as I read *In the Wilderness*, I sensed that my friend Ron DiCianni was pouring out his heart as though he were pouring paint on a canvas. With passion and great sensitivity, Ron and his co-author, Lance, share remarkable insights about suffering, always drawing from scripture and personal experience. Thank you, Ron for putting into words what I so often see you do on canvas!"

Joni Eareckson Tada,
Joni and Friends International Disability Center

If you have ever wondered where God is in the middle of formidable circumstances, this book is for you. Ron DiCianni and Lance Wubbels have given us a powerful tool for discovering that the wilderness experiences of life are stepping stones to stronger faith, renewed hope, and a vibrant future. The authors remind us that when God seems the most absent, He is the most present. Every Christian needs this book!

Carol Kent
Speaker and Author
Between a Rock and a Grace Place (Zondervan)

The Bible tells us there is "a season, and a time for every purpose under heaven." I believe *In the Wilderness* could not have come at a better time. It is an important read for every believer and follower of Jesus Christ.

It took but a few moments of reading to discover the phrase, "He gets it!" Those words lingered with me throughout the book. Could there be a clearer, simpler, or more powerful way of bringing home to our hearts the reason why Jesus, our faithful High Priest, suffered and was tempted in the wilderness?

"He gets it" in our pain and sorrow; "He gets it" in our tears and grief; "He gets it" in our weariness and weakness. No eyes can see like His; no ears can listen like His; no voice can speak like His; no thoughts can understand like His; no prayers can intercede like His; no heart can care like His. Jesus, who willingly walked into His God-appointed wilderness, can now, mercifully and tenderly, walk with us through our wilderness experience.

Roy Lessin
Co-founder
DaySpring Cards

DESTINY IMAGE BOOKS BY LANCE WUBBELS

A Time of Heroes

Bible Nobodies Who Became Somebodies

In the
WILDERNESS

*Finding God's Strength
When Your World Falls Apart*

※

Award-winning & Best-selling Authors
Ron DiCianni & Lance Wubbels

DESTINY IMAGE® PUBLISHERS, INC.
P.O. Box 310, Shippensburg, PA 17257-0310

"Promoting Inspired Lives."

This book and all other Destiny Image, Revival Press, MercyPlace, Fresh Bread, Destiny Image Fiction, and Treasure House books are available at Christian bookstores and distributors worldwide.

For a U.S. bookstore nearest you,
call 1-800-722-6774.

For more information on foreign distributors, call 717-532-3040.

Reach us on the Internet: www.destinyimage.com.

ISBN 13 TP: 978-0-7684-4216-8
ISBN 13 Ebook: 978-0-7684-8609-4

For Worldwide Distribution, Printed in the U.S.A.

1 2 3 4 5 6 7 8 / 17 16 15 14 13

DEDICATION

"To all who wonder whether you can survive
the wilderness you find yourself in."

ACKNOWLEDGMENTS

To Jesus, Who stood with me through every wilderness.

To Lance, who gave words to my voice.

"I will make the wilderness a pool of water, and the dry land springs of water" (Isaiah 41:18 NKJV).

"The Lord said, 'Go out and stand on the mountain in the presence of the Lord, for the Lord is about to pass by.' Then a great and powerful wind tore the mountains apart and shattered the rocks before the Lord, but the Lord was not in the wind. After the wind there was an earthquake, but the Lord was not in the earthquake. After the earthquake came a fire, but the Lord was not in the fire. And after the fire came a gentle whisper" (1 Kings 19:11-12).

Contents

A Wilderness Devotional

PREFACE

"There are two ways to learn from wilderness experiences. One is to endure it silently. The other is to take encouragement from others who have traveled the same path and emerged better than they went in. I hope you find the second option in this book. Someday we will celebrate together in Heaven."

Ron DiCianni

PROLOGUE

Dear fellow traveler,

It is possible we have met each other in the wilderness, but were both too weary to stop and compare notes. This book will give us a chance to do just that. Thank you for that opportunity. Hopefully as we each grow and emerge victorious from the wildernesses we encountered, we will be able to help other travelers as we watch them on their way Home.

Ron DiCianni

INTRODUCTION

As I am writing, I am looking at the program for my grandson's kindergarten play. Even now, I choke back tears as I read his name in the cast of characters—"Joseph played by Nicolas DiCianni." Nicolas is my first grandchild and best buddy. But fifteen years ago, a team of cardiac doctors informed me that I would never live long enough to see this day. It appeared my life was over. That diagnosis was the beginning of a long wilderness season in my life—one that, thankfully, concluded contrary to the dire predictions of the medical team.

What is "the wilderness"? It describes a season in life that has brought us to our knees in confused surrender. It is a season we will all enter at some point in our lives.

The biblical character Job was a man who went through the most severe wilderness experience of any person I've ever read about. He went from prosperity to poverty, happiness to hopelessness, and security to near insanity—all in one day! In the blink of an eye, his world did a complete 180. He wasn't ready for it—never saw it coming. That's the wilderness, and that may be where you find yourself today.

I have been there. Boy, have I been there. When circumstances descended upon me that were the opposite of what I thought a good God would allow, I felt scared, abandoned, alone, and confused. *Why? How? What now? Who will help me? God, please take this nightmare away!* In my pain and confusion, there was no answer and no comfort. Just deep, dark questions that seemed to fall on uncaring ears. Those times of utter silence can shake your faith—it certainly did mine.

That season of seeming isolation wasn't what I desired. In fact, my road through the wilderness with God lasted longer than I could have ever imagined. During those dark months, my questions and pain led me to some dangerous conclusions that made things even worse. God didn't give me more than I could bear, but it was way more than I wanted to bear.

When we enter into our wilderness experiences, the feelings of pain, confusion, and isolation are always the same. The only difference in each of our stories is who we allow to walk with us through the wilderness. In my case, I could have turned my back on God and made a decision to go it alone. Looking back, I would have never survived, but I realized I was in charge of my reaction to the dark night in which I found myself.

If you can identify with any of this, you may be in the wilderness right now. Your circumstances are uniquely yours, and your fears may be founded upon strong evidence, but there is good news in the middle of it all. There is GOD! You may be angry with Him or confused by what He doesn't seem to be doing to help, but fear and worry are two great impostors that need to be challenged.

In one of my wilderness moments, I read Isaiah 45:15, which at first glance seemed to make things even worse: "Truly you are a God who has been hiding himself." I immediately questioned God, "Oh, great, just when I need to see You, You play hide-and-seek." But knowing that this seemed contrary to His character, I sought a different translation that soothed my soul and gave me a new perspective. The Message reads, "Clearly, you are a God who works behind the scenes." I wept with hope when I read those words. Soon after that, through a series of events, God revealed to me that although I hadn't seen Him and oftentimes couldn't hear His voice, He was there. In fact, He had been in the wilderness with me the entire time.

When you find yourself in the wilderness, consider the possibility that the very place you are in is the exact spot where Jesus sat. He went there ahead of you. He experienced His own wilderness so He could prove to you that not only is He stronger than the wilderness, but He will even turn it for good! He not only understands what you feel and what you are going through, but He is actively, at this moment behind the scenes, working it all out for your growth and benefit. He doesn't cause the wilderness, but He most certainly will walk with you through it.

Although it may not feel like it at this moment, in the end you will not regret where you find yourself today if you hold to your faith as Job did. Eventually, the wilderness will be just a faint memory and your tears will be wiped away by His own hand. Job found that to be true. The Bible records that God blessed Job, after his wilderness, with double the blessings he had before (see Job 42:10)! God can do that for you. If you will stay close to Him through your wilderness, when you emerge you will find a new depth of understanding and spiritual growth as well as fresh power from the Holy Spirit. These are after-blessings that are forged in the fire of the wilderness. I would never have chosen to go there myself. But I am grateful for what He deposited in me as I walked *In the Wilderness.*

As you read this book, my prayer is that you, too, can find His voice in the silence. There is no need to be afraid anymore. You are not alone.

Ron DiCianni

1

INTO THE WILDERNESS

"Some wandered in desert wastelands, finding no way to a city where they could settle. They were hungry and thirsty, and their lives ebbed away. Then they cried out to the Lord in their trouble, and he delivered them from their distress" (Psalm 107:4-6).

Elizabeth was only fourteen years old, even though she looked and acted eighteen. Tall and slender, her voice, her eyes, and even the poise of her youthful figure spoke of one who had found the burden of life too heavy. She was one of the thousands of unfortunate kids who get passed from one foster home to another, always looking for love and never having found anything that even came close.

She carried a weight of suffering in the secret place of her heart that made her soul sick with hopelessness. The little dreams Elizabeth once held dear had given way to the torture of fear and dread. Finally, suicidal and full of anger, she ended up in a Christian group home in California where, for the first time, she met people who genuinely reached out to her and cared.

Sitting in the counselor's office, she was staring up at the painting *Into the Wilderness*. For the longest time, she was silent and unresponsive to the last question from the counselor. Unmindful of her surroundings, she bit her lip and leaned toward the painting as though she could unlock its meaning. Her wide questioning gaze seemed to demand that the wilderness figure tell her His thoughts.

"Elizabeth, what are you thinking about?" the counselor finally asked.

Not taking her eyes off the image of Christ in the wilderness, Elizabeth replied, "He gets it."

"Gets what?"

"He gets it, you know," she replied, finally turning her bloodshot eyes to the counselor. "He knows how I feel, even if I can't describe it to you."

The counselor smiled and nodded. "You're right about that. Do you know who He is?"

The girl's lips curved in an unconscious smile and shook her head no. "What difference does it make? He gets it. That's enough."

"Oh, He more than gets it," the counselor explained. "He gets it perfectly. Let me tell you His story."

2

To a Desolate Place

"Then Jesus was led by the Spirit into the wilderness to be tempted by the devil. After fasting forty days and forty nights, he was hungry" (Matthew 4:1-2).

"The wilderness." Just the mention of the word stands out in sheer contrast to our daily world of constant change. The wilderness is not a place where people are on the run, working round the clock, pushing and climbing and advancing to keep up with the pack. The wilderness is not concerned with having the latest, greatest iPad or cell phone or big screen television with hundreds of channels. It's not about higher salaries or more expensive homes or luxury cars.

The wilderness speaks of barrenness, dryness, emptiness, silence, loneliness, hardship, hunger, burning heat or extreme cold, waiting, wandering, and temptation. The word denotes a country not suitable for farming, without settled inhabitants and without streams of water, but having pasturage for flocks and herds. "Wilderness" was often used as a symbol of a people who had forsaken God (see Isa. 27:10), as a nation destitute of the knowledge of God (see Isa. 32:15).

The desert wilderness where the Holy Spirit led Jesus is a remarkable stretch of barren land on the eastern ridge of the Judea Mountains going by steep descents of masses of stripped bare rock down to the Dead Sea more than 1,300 feet below sea level. Because of the change in altitude, little rain falls here. The land is split by deep valleys formed by centuries of rain runoff in the mountains, and even shepherds find it difficult to live here.

This arid wilderness of twisted strata and caverns is one of the more desolate and harsh places on the earth, a solitary rocky wasteland. Hot desert winds sweep through this thirsty land, pushing the scorching heat reflected from its blistering rocks like a furnace. It is a place where loneliness is felt, a land of death. In the dark of night, its silence is deafening; the music of life has long since departed.

The words that describe this desert wilderness are similar to the words Scripture uses to describe "hell," and one can understand it being a fitting place for the devil. But why would Jesus Christ be led here for the express purpose of being tempted in a face-to-face encounter? It's especially confusing, given the context of the events of Christ's life.

Immediately preceding the temptation of Christ in the wilderness, Jesus had taken the first amazing public step into His ministry as the Messiah through His public act of John's baptism (see Matt. 3:13-17). To do so, Jesus, who never sinned or needed repentance, took His place beside sinful men, standing with and for and identifying Himself with sinners at the place of baptism.

Then the heavens were opened, and a holy dove descended from Heaven to endorse Him as the Son of God, and the Father's voice spoke from Heaven, "...This is my Son, whom I love; with him I am well pleased" (v. 17). Wonder of wonders, the long-awaited Messiah was announced with God's accompanying signs, ushering in a new dawn in the pages of history. Don't you think the people who were there were stunned? Can you imagine the buzz?

So what will God do next? How will Jesus launch His public ministry?

Rather than send His Son out to heal the sick and raise the dead and preach the Good News, the Father immediately sent Jesus into the wilderness to undergo loneliness, hunger, hardship, and temptation.

If God the Father loved Jesus, who had obeyed and loved Him perfectly, why would He lead Jesus into the wilderness to fast for forty days alone and undergo a temptation from the devil? Why?

3

How Long, O Lord, Will You Hide Your Face From Me?

"O God, you are my God, earnestly I seek you; my soul thirsts for you, my body longs for you, in a dry and weary land where there is no water" (Psalm 63:1).

Repeatedly in the Bible, we find "the wilderness" to be a place that has a dramatic impact on the lives of Old and New Testament characters. For instance,

- Moses spent forty years in the desert wilderness as a shepherd.

- The children of Israel also spent forty years wandering in the wilderness.

- The prophet Elijah escaped from Queen Jezebel into the wilderness.

- John the Baptist called for repentance in the wilderness.

- After his conversion to faith in Christ, the apostle Paul spent three years in the solitudes of Arabia before entering the tumultuous storm of his missionary life.

In many of his psalms, David also wrote about his experiences in the wilderness. It is easy to forget that the sweet psalmist of Israel and the mighty warrior and king spent years in the wilderness, first as a young shepherd, then often on the run for his life from King Saul's hatred, and later from the heartbreaking rebellion of his son Absalom. Many of his years were spent as an exile in the wilderness, and his pathways were of a wanderer and stranger.

Although David had been anointed as a young man to be king by Samuel, his way to the throne lay through years of manifold difficulties and sorrows and poverty and misery, which are expressed in his psalms.

Too often we skim or even skip over David's many anguishing words, such as:

"Why, Lord, do you stand far off? Why do you hide yourself in times of trouble? My heart pounds, my strength fails me; even the light has gone from my eyes" (Ps. 10:1; 38:10).

Perhaps we think that if we don't dwell on these painful words and whole psalms, we can avoid experiencing something similar.

"How long, Lord? Will you forget me forever? How long will you hide your face from me? How long must I wrestle with my thoughts and every day have sorrow in my heart? How long will my enemy triumph over me?" (Ps. 13:1-2)

We read these words, and they make many of us feel uncomfortable with David's honesty. Rather than embrace the words, we may try to rationalize them away. Perhaps David was having a bad day and shouldn't have been so negative.

Perhaps he'd sinned and felt this way because he needed to change his mind and move back into obedience to God. We may even feel sorry that David went through these difficult times, but one thing is for certain:

We're glad we're not in David's shoes, going through whatever was behind his words.

Until one day, we find ourselves in the wilderness in our own shoes, and the words of David suddenly become our words. We may have not chosen to come to this barren place, and we may not be ready or want to be in the wilderness, but we are here.

4

THE TASTE OF TEARS

"My God, my God, why have you forsaken me? Why are you so far from saving me, so far from my words of groaning? My God, I cry out by day, but you do not answer, by night, and am not silent" (Psalm 22:1-2).

I (Lance) was sitting toward the back of our college chapel on a bright Sunday morning, listening intently to a Bible teacher, when someone tapped me on the shoulder from behind and asked me to step out into the foyer. I followed him out, knowing from the look on his face that he was the messenger of bad news. Stepping outside the chapel, I took a deep breath as he turned to face me.

"One of the pastors just called and said that Pat and Kelly McIntosh have requested that you come with them to the hospital," he spoke quietly, shaking his head. "It's not good. Their baby is dying, and they want you to be with them when he passes."

That was over thirty years ago, and the memory is still raw. I remember walking out of the foyer to meet them at the car, searching my soul for something comforting to say, something profound that my dear friends could cling to. But everything that whirled through my head, including dozens of Scriptures, seemed so trite. What could possibly help them at this moment?

My wife and I had been classmates of Pat and Kelly at the college of missions, and we became close friends as they made preparations to go to Indonesia as missionaries. They had one sweet little boy named Shawn, whose birth had several complications. Then, after having suffered many painful miscarriages, Pat had gotten pregnant again and everything went well for the first six months. It was the fulfillment of hundreds of prayers and the joy of their souls. Shawn would have a little brother or sister to be his playmate wherever they went on the mission field.

However, on Thanksgiving Day 1979, Pat suddenly went into labor, and baby Sheldon arrived two months prematurely. Had there been any hint of a problem, the doctors would have given Sheldon shots to help prepare his lungs to develop. But there were no warnings, and despite the best medical care available, his lungs were not ready. Day after day the forced oxygen took its toll, drying out his lungs, and by the tenth agonizing day, the call from the hospital came that he wouldn't make it through the morning.

I remember stepping out of the foyer into the crisp, sun-sweet air of that gorgeous late fall morning, with warm slanting rays of sunlight falling softly through shimmering golds and brilliant yellows and flaming scarlet leaves and a filmy veil of blue haze overhead, and wondering how nature could be so nearly perfect as contrasted to the indescribable grief already etched in lines across my two friends' faces. Day after day of almost no sleep and constant anxiety had taken its toll on them, and now this—the end.

Nothing made sense. These two dear people loved God with all their hearts and had spent five years faithfully preparing to be missionaries. They were leaving their families and friends and careers and retirement plans behind to take the Gospel into a predominately Muslim nation, risking their lives for the sake of Jesus. So many people had prayed for Pat to make it through to full term and deliver a healthy child.

I wish I could say that all those prayers were answered that morning. I wish I could say that Sheldon made an amazing recovery and has graduated from college and is married today. I wish I could say that at least I found the perfect words for my friends. But none of my wishes came true that day.

All I can say is that I was there as they took that dear tiny blue baby into their arms and held him tight to their chests, with breaking hearts. I was at their sides, with a heart that broke for them. And I wept with them. We wept and wept and wept some more. We wept for hours. Over three decades later, it remains one of the most difficult experiences of my life.

To a certain degree, it reminded me of what our Lord Jesus experienced when He came to the tomb of his friend Lazarus. Seeing His friend Mary weeping and the other Jews weeping, and being "deeply moved in spirit and troubled.... Jesus wept" (John 11:33, 35). Standing face to face with the last enemy, death, He saw the devastation of sin in destroying life and the accompanying grief and sorrow, and the result of the gash that the sight of His dead friend caused in His heart and soul was simple yet profound: *Jesus wept.* His eyes turned into a fountain of tears, and His cheeks were wet with the same tears that drop from our eyes.

However, unlike Lazarus, who was miraculously resurrected by Jesus that day, baby Sheldon passed away, having only lived for ten precious days. Just ten short days in his parents' arms, clinging to life, struggling for breath. He was a fighter, he was a McIntosh, but in the end, the sting of death was all too real, and my friends were left with empty arms. It still stings.

What do we do when the sorrow of life with suffocating pain rolls over us as fog rolls in from the sea? In the aftermath of a child's death, how do we come to terms with the fact that "every good and perfect gift is from above, coming down from the Father of the heavenly lights, who does not change like shifting shadows" (James 1:17)? There was nothing about this that felt good or perfect or from above.

Was it our faith that failed? Were we to expect a miracle and that something good was about to happen to us? Did one of us...or all of us...doubt God? Was I the unfaithful one? If I had more faith on that beautiful Sunday morning, would that have made the difference?

God has a wonderful plan for everyone's life, right? We're told He wants everyone vibrantly healthy. So what went wrong? Ten days in intensive care hooked up to a dozen life-support machines and the eventual funeral didn't seem like such a good plan.

If we are supposed to be full of joy, what do we do with the depression and anger we sometimes feel? Scream and shout? What does a parent do when the nights blend into days with a haunting sorrow that seems to never end?

We never thought we would pray these words from King David until we stepped alongside of him and took our place in the wilderness:

"My tears have been my food day and night, while men say to me all day long, 'Where is your God?'" (Ps. 42:3)

We knew the taste of tears, and though we did not say it at the time, it was hard to not wonder where God was.

5

PATHWAYS
TO THE WILDERNESS

In the wilderness, we wonder. In the wilderness, we weep.

—Michael Card

Before you say, "I'm in the wilderness right now," understand that the wilderness is not defined as merely a bad day or even a bad week. It is not the parking ticket or the poor grade in a class that was unjustifiably given to you. It is not the neighbor who snubbed you after you were so nice to them. Those are, for the most part, minor irritants of everyday life that can hurt, but after a few tears or being upset for a while, you deal with them and move on.

What defines the wilderness is far more traumatic.

The pathways that lead to the wilderness come in many forms, and we seldom realize we are on a wilderness path until we're well down the trail. It often starts with a painful circumstance and the loss of something precious to us. And as we walk through the aftermath of our loss, we find ourselves in a wilderness, suddenly alone and feeling unprepared to face it.

Our path to the wilderness might be through the loss of a loved one and the closing of the casket on someone whom you never imagined you could live without.

Perhaps it involves the extreme disappointment one feels by the betrayal of a dear friend or business associate.

It's when your dear child shows signs that something is not quite right, and the doctors scratch their heads and say, "We should run more tests."

The loss of a job or a career brings a staggering blow, filling one's head with doubts about one's abilities as well as fear about the loss of finances or even possessions.

It's when the note from your spouse reads, "I'm sorry, but I just don't love you anymore. I have found someone new."

Perhaps an accident has shattered one's dreams and desires.

The loss of one's reputation due to lies and slander can wipe out in a moment what has taken a lifetime to build.

No one can define what makes a wilderness for you. Some people have great tolerance for pain, but others don't. Some individuals can remain calm and even smile through adversity, while others fall apart quickly and wear their "heart on their sleeve." However, if what you are struggling with is choking the very life out of you, or you feel as though the events that have transpired are life altering and beyond your control, that sounds as though you're in the wilderness. Experience teaches that you'll know when you're in the wilderness. It will be as obvious to you as a tack put on your seat. You'll know when it's there.

One of the ways I (Ron) was led into the wilderness came at a moment when I felt as though the sun went down on my soul. I was forty-five years old and had gone to the doctor for a routine examination, but I could tell something wasn't "routine" by the way the doctor was acting. I recall staring into the eyes of my doctor, trying to be calm, but I could feel the tension building in my throat and the pounding of my heart. I was conscious of my shallow labored breaths when the grim pronouncement came,

"You've got heart disease, Ron. Three blocked arteries."

Before the thought, *This can't be happening to me!* could begin to sink in, that blow was followed by a secondary blast that took my breath away:

"You've got thirty days to have surgery, or you're putting your life on the line."

It was as though the sharp blow of a gavel had sounded, and the pronouncement was reverberating through the room: "Dead!"

"Life is but a breath..."
so the Bible says.
Take a deep breath,
and fill your lungs.
Like an exhaled breath
that touches the freezing wintry air,
shimmers and dances in the morning light
for a moment...and is gone,
so am I.

Poof.

When your brain goes numb, thirty days barely gives you time to ask God, "Why?" How do you wrap your conscious thoughts around making plans that could involve dying within a month? On top of that, I was absolutely certain that I would not survive the "all-out invasive surgery" the medical personnel wanted me to have.

I remember sitting at the kitchen table some mornings later, tears cascading down my cheeks and dropping into my bowl of corn flakes while my wife, Pat, the love of my life, cried into her cereal bowl as well. Through the blinding tears and choked words, I was doing my best to tell her where all the important papers were kept. It was a moment we will never forget.

Fortunately, by the grace of God the doctor agreed to do two lesser procedures, even though he made it painfully clear that many people die during even the lesser operation. My thirty-day life sentence was commuted, and I've been given a highly treasured extension on life. I count every day, every week, every month, and every year as a special gift from God.

But the sweet reprieve did not keep me from entering my own personal wilderness of wondering and weeping. While heart disease was not a pathway I would have ever chosen, I discovered that my journey toward Heaven included at least one more visit to the wilderness.

God withdraws every remnant of sweetness so that the soul, in dry faith alone, may cling to the feet of Him whom it knows to be hanging before it on the cross, though in the thick darkness it does not and cannot see Him.

—Robert Nash

6

WHEN FAITH
IS STAGGERED

*It is not trials that defeat us. It is confusion
that shreds our faith.*
—Dr. James Dobson

Elijah is one of the towering figures of faith in
the Old Testament. He came forward in Israel like
the lightning, powerful in word and courageous in
deed. Under King Ahab and Queen Jezebel, the
evil presence of Baal worship had proliferated in
Israel and brought tremendous moral and spiritual
corruption. It is clear from the horrible cult scene
on Mount Carmel (see 1 Kings 18) that the worship of this Tyrian deity had become entrenched as
a power in the land, with its debased and perverted
practices fueling the dark influence of Jezebel.

We are thrilled to see the splendid leader Elijah take a stand in a fierce confrontation with the 250 prophets of Baal on Mount Carmel. We hear the words of challenge from Elijah: "Call on the name of your god, and I will call on the name of the Lord. The god who answers by fire—he is God...." (v. 24). The idolatrous priests had everything in their favor, for at noon the sun god was supposed to be on his throne, but there was no voice hour after hour.

But when Elijah called on the Lord, the fire fell from Heaven, and the prophets of Baal were destroyed in a ruthless judgment. That phenomenal victory was followed by a marvelous answer to Elijah's passionate prayer for rain. Both mighty acts were a powerful call to restore the true worship of Jehovah in Israel.

However, no one saw what his rugged and raw bravery cost Elijah to accomplish these incredible wonders of God's power. But one can easily imagine the stress involved and its weakening impact on his soul as one climactic event followed right on the heels of the other. As the smoke cleared, Elijah began to come down from his pinnacle of success, and the enemy found a weakness in his armor. Elijah believed incorrectly that he was alone, and when threatened directly by Queen Jezebel, he became afraid and ran for his life (see 1 Kings 19:3, 10).

His escape took him into the desert wilderness, a barren place where the streams of water had long since dried up. His faith had been staggered, and he lost the clear perspective he had previously had of the situation. Convinced that he was abandoned and beaten, as he fled, "...He came to a broom tree, sat down under it and prayed that he might die. 'I have had enough, Lord,' he said. 'Take my life; I am no better than my ancestors.' Then he lay down under the tree and fell asleep" (v. 4).

Such are the extreme swings of human experience, from prophet/superhero to one assailed by a threat from the wicked Jezebel, standing in triumph against the powers of darkness and then driven to question his very purpose for living.

And so Elijah goes to sleep in the wilderness, his body and soul and nerves and mind and heart beyond the point of weariness, wishing his life could end.

7

FACING THE
INCOMPREHENSIBLE

*God whispers to us in our pleasures, speaks to
us in our conscience, but shouts in our pains:
It is His megaphone to rouse a deaf world.*
— C.S. Lewis

Long before the fiery prophet Elijah waged
warfare on Mount Carmel, "in the land of Uz
there lived a man whose name was Job..." (Job 1:1).
Similar to Abraham's friend Melchizedek, the king
of Salem, Job was a heroic character who possessed
a knowledge of God that came from outside the
Hebrew covenant and the mainstream of the Old
Testament revelation. Many scholars believe his
background was Arabic.

We understand Job to be a noble, renowned, and influential man. His life was marked by great prosperity, affluence, and all but boundless resources, which in the social context of life then... and now...suggested God's abundant favor. God said about Job, "...He is blameless and upright, a man who fears God and shuns evil..." (v. 8). He was such a complete character that we wonder if he's a real person. If you read Job's story, you discover that all was well in Job's life, and his faith and character were literally the talk of Heaven.

But the day came for Job to face the incomprehensible. Every man has his own battle to fight and devil to confront. Satan hit Job with multiple trials that came one after another like thunderclaps— the loss of his children, the loss of his possessions and wealth, the loss of his health, and the loss of his godly reputation. Everything in Job's life changed in a fury, and he was left alone with a wife who tells him to curse God and die (see Job 2:9).

In Job's case, we see what the devil can do. Satan thought that Job's excellent character was due to God's protection, but Job proved the devil wrong. When the trials struck and his life was

stripped to the core, Job found the strength to hold
to the first principles upon which his life rested:
"...The Lord gave and the Lord has taken away;
may the name of the Lord be praised" (Job 1:21).
Broken and crushed, Job was content to leave his
prayer in God's hands, Who knows when and what
to give, what to withhold, and what to take away.
Job whispers, "Let it be as God wills, and He will
determine what is best for me."

If you listen closely to Job's words of utter
submission to the will of God, you'll hear them
echoed by Jesus Christ in the sorrowful agony of
the Garden of Gethsemane, "Father, if you are willing, take this cup from me; yet not my will, but
yours be done" (Luke 22:42). Richard Foster has
said, "To applaud the will of God, to do the will of
God, even to fight for the will of God is not difficult...until it comes at cross-purposes with our will.
Then the lines are drawn, the debate begins, and
the self-deception takes over. But in the School of
Gethsemane we learn that 'my will, my way, my
good' must yield to a higher authority."[1]

Where most men would have crumbled, Job
remained true to God in his wilderness experience.

Nevertheless, that was but the first blast fired in the great spiritual battle that would be waged for the soul of Job, and the same is true for us. This world is not Heaven, and evil is rampant here. When Adam and Eve disobeyed and evil entered the world, it opened up Pandora's box, which has not been closed. Drunk drivers roll down the road toward us as we are taking our kids to soccer practice. Cancer afflicts the righteous and the sinner alike. Drugs cause people to do unthinkable acts toward others. People betray and hurt one another on the deepest levels. Pedophiles and sexual predators and their horrible offenses are routinely in the news headlines. Fires and earthquakes and tornadoes and hurricanes and floods take lives and properties indiscriminately.

We all must come to terms with the terrible effects of sin in this world. Bad things happen that Satan will use to inflame our doubts and weaknesses. Storms will break upon us that we never dreamed possible...and leave us in a position where we either get angry and bitter at God for not sparing us or delivering us out of trouble, or we find peace and rest by yielding ourselves to God and saying, "Not my will, but yours be done."

Dark days of confusion and despair lay ahead for Job. Though he would not curse God or charge God with wrongdoing, Job would curse the day of his birth and could find no reason to wish to stay alive (see Job 3), which we've already seen in the case of Elijah. It is hard to read about the depths of his agony: "For sighing comes to me instead of food; my groans pour out like water. What I feared has come upon me; what I dreaded has happened to me. I have no peace, no quietness; I have no rest, but only turmoil" (vv. 24-26).

Job takes his place in the wilderness—shocked, confused, suffering, and full of grief.

[God's] silence is the sign that He is bringing you into a marvelous understanding of Himself.

—Oswald Chambers

ENDNOTE

1. Richard J. Foster, *Prayer: Finding the Heart's True Home* (New York: HarperCollins Publishers, 1992), 50.

8

BURNING QUESTIONS
IN THE WILDERNESS

*Job said in the midst of his wilderness,
"Though he slay me, yet will I hope in
him..."* (Job 13:15).

Job faced dark days in his life when messenger
followed messenger with devastating news, and he
sat down in the ruins of what was once his happiness. His body was wracked with a tropical disease,
and his wife had broken faith with him. He was
horribly alone, and all the earthly pleasures and
comforts that had colored his world were gone.
Most damaging of all, he believed that what had
transpired was from God's hand, never once real-
izing that it was the devil's work.

Then came Job's friends who, despite their genuine pity for him, would try to place the blame for all that had gone wrong squarely at his feet, as a judgment of God for Job's unconfessed sins. Their attempts to comfort only lead to deepening outbursts of despair by Job and never came close to touching the source of his pain. If he wasn't in the wilderness before they came, they certainly brought it with them.

From the story of Job, we know the wilderness is filled with burning questions:

- Why me?

- What have I done to deserve this?

- Have I sinned?

- Is God mad at me?

- Where is God?

- Why can't I find a way out of this?

- I pray, but answers don't come.

- I feel as though God has me on "hold," and I don't know how long it's going to be before He comes back on the line.

- I wish I could do something, yet God gives no direction.

- I don't know which way to go, so I wander, feeling completely lost or numb. I feel paralyzed.

- My life may be in chaos, yet I am at a loss as to what I can do to change things.

- Worst of all, I do not feel God's presence or see His hand in my life.

- I take the precious Bible and read its words, hoping to find the life and strength I need to keep going, but I can't find the meaning and comfort I once did. Honestly, I feel absolutely nothing.

- Loved ones, friends, and other believers bring little joy to my heart and don't understand what's wrong with me. Why should they? I don't understand.

IN THE WILDERNESS

- There seems to be no action I can take and no truth that makes a difference.

- I pray by faith, but my heart is cold and empty.

- Feelings of resignation frighten me.

- The wilderness is a silent place, a dark place. I hate it.

9

WHY GOD?

*"Is it nothing to you, all you who pass by?
Look around and see. Is any suffering like
my suffering that was inflicted on me, that
the Lord brought on me in the day of his
fierce anger? From on high he sent fire,
sent it down into my bones. He spread a
net for my feet and turned me back. He
made me desolate, faint all the day long"*
(Lamentations 1:12-13).

As with the prophet Jeremiah, sometimes
the wilderness is so barren or lasts so long that we
begin to despair. We cannot imagine why God is
doing or allowing things in the manner they are
unfolding. Nothing makes sense. We may try to
rationalize the path our life has taken, but often

this is impossible. We look at others whose lives seem so bright, and we wonder where we failed.

In the dryness of the wilderness, any sense of tangible assurance has been wiped away. We can't seem to reclaim what we once thought were certainties. Outwardly, we trudge on, but deep within we are haunted with thoughts of what's wrong with us.

- Has God abandoned me?

- Do I truly love God? Did I...ever... really love God?

- If I remain faithful, why is He distant?

- Why do my prayers remain unanswered?

- Have I lost my faith?

- Will I ever experience joy again?

Against the backdrop of the wilderness, we may be thinking, *God, I'll hang in there, because You'll come through for me.* We try to force a faith key into the mix and move the hand of God, or when that doesn't work, we try to negotiate with Him. When God does not eventually come through for us, some of us suffer depression, anxiety, or overwhelming anger. In the depths of our life, the truth is that we're not asking for God's will to be done. We don't want to hear Him whisper, "No. Give it up. That's not My way for you. Let it go."

We want to run, but where do we go? We weep because the pain is great, and we feel we have no one to whom we can turn. It seems as though God has left us alone to deal with a situation we are powerless to handle. Worst of all, it feels as if it will never end—this is now our lot in life. In private moments, we may wish we had never been born.

> When pain is to be borne, a little courage helps more than much knowledge, a little human sympathy more than much courage, and the least tincture of the love of God more than all.
>
> —C.S. Lewis

10

THE EXPERIENCE OF CHRIST
IN THE WILDERNESS

"For we do not have a high priest who is unable to empathize with our weaknesses, but we have one who has been tempted in every way, just as we are—yet was without sin" (Hebrews 4:15).

So why must we experience the wilderness? What purpose does it serve? What does the experience of Jesus in the wilderness teach us about our experience?

"Jesus was led by the Spirit into the wilderness to be tempted by the devil" (Matt. 4:1). The Greek word for *tempted* or *tried* means to be tested to the full extent of Satan's power. It was God's will that this mighty battle should be fought in the wilderness. The Messiah had come to crush Satan, destroy his works, and to set up the Kingdom of God among men (see 1 John 3:8). And Satan, the prince of hell's kingdom, would strike Him with all his cunning and power.

The wilderness battle was fought for forty days, and Jesus did not eat until it was over. Three specific incidents are recorded in detail, but the temptation should not be restricted to the end of the forty days. Jesus endured temptation for the entire forty days, and through His experiences here as well as throughout the rest of His life, He was tempted "in every way" as we are. This does not mean that every particular temptation came to Jesus, but the essence of every temptation. How otherwise could He be our High Priest and Savior in every sense of those terms?

We tend to forget that Jesus was both fully God and fully man. Because He was truly a man, He was subject to the same desires that lure our hearts. Jesus had to pass through the full range of human experience, with its highest joys and deepest sorrows. He must battle the devil and defeat his subtlest temptations and heaviest assaults. He must endure hunger, thirst, physical pain, and hardship so that He may experience the problems that we face.

Until He went through these experiences, He did not *know* our human experience. It is one thing to know about something, and another thing to experience and know it in reality. We know only with certainty those things we experience. Personal experience wields truth and knowledge into the structure of our life. It tests and proves what is most precious to us, so dear as to be our very life. For instance, the three young Hebrews knew and made a public confession that God had the power to rescue their lives, but they did not *know* if He would until they stepped into the super-heated furnace (see Dan. 3). We *know* only what we experience.

Jesus became a perfect man by means of the experiences He went through. Through this process, there is nothing lacking in the character and person of Christ to keep Him from being able to save us: "In bringing many sons and daughters to glory, it was fitting that God, for whom and through whom everything exists, should make the pioneer of their salvation perfect through suffering" (Heb. 2:10).

How did Jesus suffer? *Temptation* is called *suffering* in Hebrews 2:18: "Because he himself suffered when he was tempted, he is able to help those who are being tempted." The word for both *temptation* and *trial* is the same in the Bible. Jesus' experiences brought Him cutting pain, real suffering in being tried, including fervent cries and tears (see Heb. 5:7). From His earliest consciousness until His ultimate suffering and death on the cross, Jesus went through the whole range of human experiences common to us all.

Hebrews 5:8 adds that "Although he [Jesus] was a son, he learned obedience from what he suffered." Such an amazing statement is so hard to comprehend. As a man, our Savior had to learn. He was of a teachable spirit, who always did what His Father showed Him, and by His sufferings the Lord was made to know to the fullest extent what obedience means. His was a practical, personal acquaintance with obedience; and in all this He comes very near to us. He obeyed every step of the way, "and became obedient to death— even death on a cross!" (Phil. 2:8).

Through His experience in the wilderness as well as throughout His life, Jesus Christ was thus prepared to accomplish mankind's redemption. Being made perfect through suffering, He is able to fully carry out His office as Savior. He has suffered to the end all that was needed to make Him our Messiah. There is nothing lacking in Him. At every point essential to our salvation, Jesus is perfect.

Jesus went to the wilderness, conquered Satan and what the world had to offer Him by His utter resignation to obeying His Father's will, and showed us how to do the same. Based on His example, there is no way we can ever go to God and say, "You don't know how this feels. You don't know how deep this hurts." He knows every feeling that it's possible to feel, and every situation that we face. And because He successfully conquered the wilderness, He imparts divine strength for us to conquer our own wilderness, if we will take it. By His grace and power, we can become part of the solution to our wilderness by always surrendering our lives to Him, trusting in Him, hoping in Him, and doing what we know to be right.

11

THE CALL
OF THE WILDERNESS

*"Then Jesus said to his disciples, 'If anyone
would come after me, he must deny himself and take up his cross and follow me'"*
(Matthew 16:24).

*"To this you were called, because Christ suf-
fered for you, leaving you an example, that
you should follow in his steps"* (1 Peter 2:21).

If Jesus must go through the wilderness experience, how much more those of us who follow in
His steps? Jesus took a mighty stride in His preparation to face the cross when He was in the wilderness. He fought the enemy there, won a mighty
battle, and was ready for the difficulties that lay
ahead for His ministry.

Anyone who loves God and desires to fulfill His will for his or her life will experience the wilderness. However, the wilderness is not a place or a time to fear, because when it comes, it is no accident. Although we may not understand what God is doing when He leads us to a desert place of difficult circumstances, spiritual dryness, or sorrow and pain, we should never conclude it is purposeless. As difficult as the wilderness may be, it is one of the significant places where God works His purposes in our life. God often uses the wilderness to bring us to a place that He wants us to go because there's no other way to get us there.

The apostle James was clear that our spiritual growth or maturity in Christ demands the difficulties that are associated with the wilderness. He wrote: "Consider it pure joy, my brothers, whenever you face trials of many kinds, because you know that the testing of your faith develops perseverance. Perseverance must finish its work so that you may be mature and complete, not lacking anything" (James 1:2-4).

The call of the wilderness is to a deeper place of faith, where we learn to depend on God in new ways. It can come because our loving Father desires to enter a new dimension in our relationship with Him. God longs for us to be conformed to the image of Jesus Christ at the center of our being, and the wilderness provides a place for inner transformation. "For those God foreknew he also predestined to be conformed to the likeness of his Son, that he might be the firstborn among many brothers" (Rom. 8:29).

That deeper place of faith is always connected to prayer. "Do not be anxious about anything," said the apostle Paul, who was a veteran of wilderness experiences, "but in everything, by prayer and petition, with thanksgiving, present your requests to God. And the peace of God, which transcends all understanding, will guard your hearts and your minds in Christ Jesus" (Phil. 4:6-7). Oswald Chambers adds, "Have you been propping up that foolish soul of yours with the idea that your circumstances are too much for God to handle? Set all your opinions and speculations aside and 'abide under the shadow of the Almighty' (see Ps. 91:1). Deliberately tell God that you will not fret about whatever concerns you. All our fretting and worrying is caused by planning without God."[1] Prayer is the first order of getting through the wilderness.

The wilderness can be a season in our life when God strips us of things that keep us from going further in our walk with Him. It might be that there are bad habits or issues of sin that need to be exposed to the light and repentance needs to follow. Perhaps the external props and the trappings of faith are removed, and internal comforts are suspended. We discover or are reminded that "good itself does not dwell" in our flesh (see Rom. 7:18) and that any claims we make to true spirituality are vain. Into our emptiness, God pours the pure life of His Holy Spirit and changes us into the image of His precious Son.

It may be that our wilderness experience is a teaching period, a time to stop and listen to what God is speaking to us. One of the hardest lessons for the human heart is to renounce self-dependence and trust wholly in Christ. Some of us feel that He should be giving us something different than what we're experiencing in the wilderness. We may even try to prescribe to God what He shall direct and bless, and when and how.

If we could hear God whisper, we might find that He's saying, "What is it about no that you don't understand?" We need a paradigm shift that embraces God's sovereign Lordship over us. He will come in His own way, and we must never limit His working. Perhaps He is asking us to give up our own plans and agendas in exchange for what He has for us—to "die to self." It may be a time of testing to discover whether we are willing to accept His will in all things.

Perhaps we are being prepared for something that God has in store for us. As with Jesus' temptation in the wilderness, our preparation may involve an intense spiritual warfare with the enemy of our souls. We cannot be taught lessons in life's battles or deal with grief or loss merely by reading books or discussing them in the classroom or with friends, as helpful and as good as those may be. Obedience for us, as it was for Jesus, is learned only by actually doing the divine will, which includes suffering. This is our time of schooling and discipline, and we are learning to love and obey God, which is the highest and best of all lessons.

In his book *How to Handle Adversity*, Charles Stanley says, "If our lives are free from pain, turmoil, and sorrow, our knowledge of God will remain purely academic. There would always be a sense of distance and mystery. This is not the kind of relationship God wants with His children... God is in the process of engineering circumstances through which He can reveal Himself to each of us. And both history as well as our personal testimonies bear witness to the fact that it is in times of adversity that we come to a greater realization of God's incredible faithfulness to us."[2]

Holding on to faith in the heat of the wilderness, listening for His voice in the silent darkness, clinging to hope in the midst of turmoil and anguish, we learn to endure, to press through. One day the light will dawn on our soul. Tried by fire, our "...faith—of greater worth than gold, which perishes even though refined by fire—may be proved genuine and result in praise, glory and honor when Jesus Christ is revealed" (1 Pet. 1:7). As was the case with Abraham and the surrender he was asked to make of his son, Isaac, we may be severely put to the test, yet come to hear the Angel of the Covenant's marvelous commendation, "...Now I know that you fear God, because you have not withheld from me your son, your only son" (Gen. 22:12).

In the wilderness, God calls us to a complete abandonment or surrender to Him, holding nothing back. When we are left with the living God alone, we begin to see Him as He really is. We are weaned from a dependence on the tangible experiences of His presence and rooted deeper in His unconditional infinite love, which He imprints more fully upon our heart, conforming us more to the image of Christ. It is the difference between knowing about God and truly knowing Him.

Job said that before his wilderness experience, he talked about God but didn't really understand Him. After all he faced, Job said, "My ears had heard of you but now my eyes have seen you" (Job 42:5).

ENDNOTES

1. Oswald Chambers, *My Utmost for His Highest* (Uhrichsville, OH: Barbour Publishing, Inc., 1935, 1963), July 4.

2. Charles Stanley, *How to Handle Adversity* (Nashville: Thomas Nelson, 1989), ch. 12.

12

STRENGTH OF CHARACTER

"The real problem is not why some pious, humble, believing people suffer, but why some do not."

—C.S. Lewis

"If you falter in a time of trouble, how small is your strength!" (Proverbs 24:10)

The reality is that many of us are not well-prepared for the wilderness. We are not a generation of believers who have been taught what it means to suffer with Christ or for what Dietrich Bonhoeffer called *The Cost of Discipleship*. Many of our churches and ministries put a premium emphasis on what most people want to hear, as though God is a divine ATM machine, where we punch in our requests and receive what we ask instantly. Many of us want God to fulfill our dreams in Disneyland

fashion and are upset when God puts us on hold...
let alone leads us into the wilderness. We are so in
love with this world that we cannot give it up.

Many of us have bought into the notion that
we deserve "happiness" and luxury and ease as
though God has promised those to us, but God
doesn't owe us anything. When life brings difficult
circumstances and hard times, we feel afraid and
out of control and demand that God change things
in our favor. In today's culture, we're not driven as
much by what we believe as by what we feel, and
because the wilderness experience often sends our
feelings reeling in a thousand different directions,
it's as though we are being put through a paper
shredder with no way out. When we start with a
mindset that our life should be a bed of roses, we
are not just asking for disappointment but are
bound for disappointment.

Too little emphasis, or even no emphasis, is
given to our character development as children
of God by our loving Father's discipline in our
lives. The writer of Hebrews says, "Endure hardship as discipline; God is treating you as sons.
For what son is not disciplined by his father?...

Our fathers disciplined us for a little while as they thought best; but God disciplines us for our good, that we may share in his holiness. No discipline seems pleasant at the time, but painful. Later on, however, it produces a harvest of righteousness and peace for those who have been trained by it" (Heb. 12:7, 10-11).

The special object of all the Father's training and discipline through which we pass in life, including the wilderness experience, is the increase of strength of character. The storms and darkness and troubles of life are to be accepted as a preparation for higher service, for more patient endurance, that we might share God's holiness. Oswald Chambers said, "The destined end of man is not happiness, nor health, but holiness. God's one aim is the production of saints."[1] How unfortunate it is when we miss the lessons of the wilderness—the life of Jesus developed in us—because we refuse to submit and yield to the Father's hand.

The writer of Proverbs 24:10 used no introductory words for "a time of trouble" or "the day of adversity," for we understand the meaning instantly. Every life has its day of adversity or a time of trouble—it is our universal experience. Some lives, in fact, seem to experience far greater trials, troubles, disappointments, sorrows, and pains than others. The strongest person experiences bitter hours of intense pain and agony in the wilderness.

It is in the time of trouble that our strength of character is tested. We do not know our personal mettle until we have fallen into "trials of many kinds" (James 1:2). I once heard Ravi Zacharias repeat what he said was an old Indian proverb, "When you are bumped, what spills out is what was in there the whole time." The day of adversity is the scorching heat of the wilderness that reveals what's been inside of us the whole time—what our character really is. We may think we know ourselves and talk a good talk, but how do we fare when the clouds of distress and pain gather and storms break upon us? Sometimes the masquerade that we live, or the things that we do when everything's going well, may not really be what's deep down inside. We don't truly know ourselves until we have been tested—our emotions torn, our hopes turned to disappointment, our joy to bitterness.

The wilderness can't force us to change what we discover is wrong in our lives, but it can force us to at least look at them and then to make a decision regarding the kind of person we want to become from that moment forward. We are either better or worse off for the trials through which we pass. We either allow the experiences to harden our heart or to make us more Christlike.

To *falter* or *faint* in the time of trouble is to distrust God. When the winds are beating upon us, we must not allow it to shake our confidence in God. Jesus asks only one thing: "Remain in me, and I will remain in you..." (John 15:4). Faith sustains and comforts and refines us. It gives value to suffering, a new meaning to dark circumstances and pain; and while faith may not elevate us to the point of praise and triumph, it enables us to stay in our Father's hands and offer a grand expression of worship: "Your will be done!"

When the whole world seemed to be collapsing around Job and his life must have felt like one terrible desolation, he found the honesty and courage to say about God, "When he is at work in the north, I do not see him; when he turns to the south, I catch no glimpse of him. But he knows the way that I take; when he has tested me, I will come forth as gold" (Job 23:9-10). Those are powerful words for us to remember in the wilderness.

The prophet Habakkuk came along hundreds of years later and faced despair as he watched a dark chapter of disaster overtake the land of Judah. Where, he asks, is God? Why does He allow evil to triumph? Why, God? Yet in the midst of his agony over human pain, Habakkuk said, "Though the fig tree does not bud and there are no grapes on the vines, though the olive crop fails and the fields produce no food, though there are no sheep in the pen and no cattle in the stalls, yet I will rejoice in the Lord, I will be joyful in God my Savior" (Hab. 3:17-18). Here was a man who knew his way through the wilderness!

Peter had declared, "...Lord, I am ready to go with you to prison and to death" (Luke 22:33), but he had to have a bitter denial of Christ experience before he became the Peter who fearlessly led the New Testament church after Pentecost. In Peter's wilderness before the resurrection, you know that he thought day and night about every facet of his failure. Tradition says that whenever, in the coming years, Peter heard a cock crow, he was accustomed to fall on his knees and weep. While this may not be a correct version of the subsequent expression of his repentance, it is an appropriate expression that his strong, boastful spirit had received its death wound.

And what of the apostle Paul when he cried out repeatedly to God for deliverance from a tormenting "thorn in my flesh," yet God said to him, "My grace is sufficient for you, for my power is made perfect in weakness" (2 Cor. 12:7, 9)? If God does not take away the thorn, He provides the sufficient grace and power in our weakness. Paul went on to rejoice in his weaknesses for that very reason. Nothing can break the darkness of such days but the light of God's Word; nothing can heal such wounds but the balm of the grace of the cross of Christ.

God grant that when we find ourselves in the wilderness, and the tempter or his co-workers come upon us with cunning to confuse and deceive, we too may find the light and the strength to endure and overcome through Him who loves us!

When we have hit bottom and are emptied of all we thought important to us, then we truly pray....In the midst of the emptying, we know that God hasn't deserted us. He has merely removed the obstacles keeping us from a deeper union with Him. —Brennan Manning

ENDNOTE

1. Oswald Chambers, *My Utmost for His Highest* (Uhrichsville, OH: Barbour Publishing, Inc., 1935, 1963), September 1.

13

WHEN WE DO NOT SEE

Your thoughts of God are too human.

—Martin Luther

"For my thoughts are not your thoughts, neither are your ways my ways," declares the Lord. "As the heavens are higher than the earth, so are my ways higher than your ways and my thoughts than your thoughts" (Isaiah 55:8-9).

In the wilderness, we are humbled before God. We begin to see how small and powerless we are on our own. For in the wilderness, there is nothing we can do to make a difference or change a situation, when God determines it so. When we try, we fail, feeling more helpless than before. In the wilderness we come to understand that God alone is God—there is no other—and that there are mysteries in our walk with Him that are beyond explanation...and perhaps will *never* be understood here on earth.

I've heard it said that it's OK to admit that we cannot come up with solutions to all of life's complications. When we reach our last days, we choose to trust the power and wisdom of God.

Being in a wilderness of pain and confusion and the loss of precious comforts erodes any notion that God's ways are comprehensible to our finite minds. Too often we try to humanize God and shape Him in our own image, as though we can grasp His sovereignty. To do so blinds us to the truth that He does what He knows is best for us, even if it baffles and defies every reasoning we can imagine.

Maybe that's what rubs us the wrong way where God is concerned. Because we can't figure Him out and force Him to conform to our expectations, we come to the conclusion He just doesn't understand or care. In fact, it is just the opposite, isn't it? It's us who just don't understand Him! Our refusal to let God be God gives us shivers up our spine and a tantrum of sarcasm or harsh words that reflect our ignorance, not His.

God will not conform to our expectations, be guided by us, or be limited to our finite perspective of what is happening. He is aware of our desires and requests, but He sees the bigger plan, the whole plan. He sees what our eyes cannot see and our minds cannot understand. God's call to us in the wilderness may be to "let go" of what we want or what we think is best for us and to release our need to understand. That can be a very difficult pill for us to swallow.

David said, "My heart is not proud, O Lord, my eyes are not haughty; I do not concern myself with great matters or things too wonderful for me. But I have stilled and quieted my soul, like a weaned child with its mother, like a weaned child is my soul within me" (Ps. 131:1-2). In the wilderness, we learn to rest in the Father's love and care, no matter how unfathomable we perceive the situation. This perspective is our hope, and hope in God is never wasted hope. God never ever fails.

In the solitude of the wilderness, God calls to us: "Who among you fears the Lord and obeys the word of his servant? Let him who walks in the dark, who has no light, trust in the name of the Lord and rely on his God" (Isa. 50:10). If we find ourselves walking in a pitch-black place, we must trust, rely upon, put our confidence in, hope in God—nothing else matters here. We come to grips with the fact that "faith is being sure of what we hope for and certain of what we do not see" (Heb. 11:1).

In her book *The God of All Comfort*, Hannah Whithall Smith says, "We may find ourselves in a 'wilderness' of disappointment and suffering, and we wonder why the God who loves us should have allowed it. But He knows that it is only in that very uncomfortable wilderness that we can hear and receive the 'comfortable words' He has to pour out upon us. We must feel the need of comfort before we can listen to the words of comfort. And God knows that it is infinitely better and happier for us to need His comforts and receive them, than it could ever be not to need them and so be without them. The consolations of God mean the substituting of a far higher and better thing for what we lose to get them."[1]

Perhaps we have learned the wilderness's most "comfortable" lesson when we are able to honestly say, "Almighty God, I love You. You are all I need." It is not about what God might do or how He might make us feel or what He might give us. We lay aside what He has done or how we have felt or what we have received. We release our demand for the sense of His presence or the benefits of His kindness. We seek God for Himself alone... for He is enough.

> Christ has not been all we want. We have wanted a great many things besides Him. We have wanted fervent feelings about Him, or realizations of His presence with us, or an interior revelation of His love; or else we have demanded satisfactory schemes of doctrine, or successful Christian work, or something of one sort or another, besides Himself, that will constitute as personal claim upon Him. Just Christ Himself, Christ alone, without the addition of any of our experiences concerning Him, has not been enough for us in spite of all our singing; and we do not even see how it is possible

that He could be enough. —Hannah Whithall Smith[2]

ENDNOTES

1. Hannah Whitall Smith, *The God of All Comfort and the Secret of His Comforting* (London: James Nisbet & Co., 1906), 35.

2. Ibid., 246.

14

THIS IS NOT
THE END OF THE STORY

*The parental heart of God has no desire to
hurt us. But He understands that we must
get our priorities straight. We cry. We pout.
We sigh and groan. We say unkind things
about God. He does not intervene. He lets
us continue through the process. And we are
saved. A little grief has spared us a much
greater sorrow. We can only conclude that
God is good, that He is tender and compas-
sionate even when we feel that we have a
right to complain that He is unkind.*

—Fenelon

Knowing we are in the wilderness, and real-
izing it is part of God's redeeming work in our
lives, can make a tremendous difference in our

experience. Rather than hoping it will end or even fighting against it, knowing His plan not only steadies us through the toughest moments of faith but enables us to actually embrace the wilderness, despite the difficulties.

The apostle James encourages us to follow in the footsteps of the Old Testament prophets and Job in the wilderness: "Brothers and sisters, as an example of patience in the face of suffering, take the prophets who spoke in the name of the Lord. As you know, we consider blessed those who have persevered. You have heard of Job's perseverance and have seen what the Lord finally brought about. The Lord is full of compassion and mercy" (James 5:10-11).

One person who lived James's words and persevered in a dire wilderness place was Horatio Spafford, a successful lawyer in Chicago and a personal friend of the nineteenth-century evangelist Dwight Moody. In the wake of the great Chicago fire in 1871, despite heavy losses of real estate investments and the recent death of their son, Spafford and his wife, Anna, dedicated themselves to helping those who had been impoverished by the devastating fire, which they did tirelessly.

Spafford and his family decided to go to England in November 1873 to join Moody and Ira Sankey on an evangelistic crusade and then take a well-earned vacation in Europe. The Spaffords and their four daughters booked passage on the French steamship *Ville de Havre*, sailing from New York. However, when Spafford was delayed by business, he sent his wife and daughters ahead and planned to join them later.

At the last moment Spafford changed their stateroom from amidships to near the bow of the vessel. Anna and the girls sailed, and off the coast of Newfoundland, their ship was struck by the English sailing ship *Lochearn* and sank in twelve minutes. Had they been in their original stateroom, all would have been killed. As it was, Anna and the four little girls were cast into the harsh icy waters. She frantically tried to save the girls, but all four drowned in the inky black sea. Anna was found floating unconscious on a piece of wreckage and was rescued. Only 47 of the 226 passengers survived.

Several days later the survivors landed at Cardiff, Wales, and Anna Spafford cabled her husband the brief message, "Saved alone." One can hardly imagine what he must have felt when he received these words. He immediately dropped all business and boarded the next ship so he could be with his bereaved wife.

As the ship was en route, the captain called Spafford to the bridge. Pointing to a chart, the captain told him that they were passing near the spot where the *Ville de Havre* had sunk. Crushed by the sorrow, Spafford walked the deck alone, but he was overtaken by a sense of peace as he realized that he would see his daughters again in Heaven. Watching the waves rolling on the ocean, he recalled the words of the Lord, "I will extend peace to her like a river..." (Isa. 66:12), and penned the lyrics to one of the most beloved hymns in Christian history, "It Is Well With My Soul."[1] In the midst of his sorrow, he wrote these unforgettable words that have brought solace to so many in grief:

This Is Not the End of the Story

When peace like a river, attendeth my way,
When sorrows like sea billows roll;
Whatever my lot, Thou hast taught me to say,
It is well, it is well with my soul.

Though Satan should buffet,
though trials should come,
Let this blest assurance control,
That Christ has regarded my helpless estate,
And hath shed His own blood for my soul.

My sin, oh, the bliss of this glorious thought!
My sin, not in part but the whole,
Is nailed to the cross, and I bear it no more,
Praise the Lord, praise the Lord, O my soul!

And, Lord, haste the day
when my faith shall be sight,
The clouds be rolled back as a scroll;
The trump shall resound,
and the Lord shall descend,
Even so, it is well with my soul.

As was true of Job in the Old Testament, in the midst of a barren wilderness of the soul, Spafford experienced the reality that though God does not exempt us from suffering, He is always with us in and through our times of suffering. Both men saw "the bigger picture." They believed that God is sovereign, and that He knows what He is doing even when it is completely unexplainable to us. Both men lived their lives for a time and place that was bigger than this temporary earth. Because of their faith, they could say, "This is not the end of the story. I will see my children and the goodness of God again, for my hope doesn't depend on what I experience here. I will believe and draw strength from the Word of God, even when my heart is breaking."

Never let yourself succumb to feelings of Divine betrayal, which is Satan's most effective tool against us. Instead, store away your questions for a lengthy conversation on the other side, and then press on toward the mark.

—Dr. James Dobson

ENDNOTE

1. *Lutheran Book of Worship* (Minneapolis: Augsburg Publishing House, 1978), 346, "When Peace, like a River."

15

Beware of "If" in the Wilderness

Temptations discover what we are.
—Thomas à Kempis

So what do we do in the wilderness? How do we not only survive but be strengthened through our experience there? Again, we gain tremendous insight from the example of Jesus Christ. Everything He revealed to us while He was in the wilderness will help us through our own wilderness.

First, let us do away with the notion that the wilderness or a season of heavy temptation is because of personal sin. The confusing thoughts and emotions we feel in the wilderness push many of us to believe that our situation is a punishment from God for sin. As was true in Job's situation, it is even possible that our loved ones and trusted friends may tell us that what we are going through must be because we have unconfessed sin in our life. Anyone with a sensitive heart is already prone to thinking he or she is a bad person and deserves it.

Remember, Jesus was "led" by the Holy Spirit into the wilderness. The temptation was a part of a plan, not an accident. He was tempted and tested severely, and there was no trace of sin in His life.

Beware of the message that comes to you in the wilderness with an attachment that starts with "If." Notice the point of attack was our Lord's Sonship: "*If* you are the Son of God." The primary target Satan aims at through temptation is to interfere in and disrupt our relationship to God as our Father, and so to cut off our dependence on and our communion with Him.

Satan implies that "if" Jesus really is the Son of God, the Father would never allow Him to be in such a difficult position. Either God is not Jesus' Father, or He is a very unkind one, and Jesus needs to take action on His own. To experience sufferings, troubles, and pains are the substantial arguments that Satan uses to get us to question our sonship; as if the allowing of afflictions and difficulties are not consistent with God's fatherly love. He paints pictures of God to appear as unkind or unfaithful, who will forsake or forget those who have given their all to Him.

Never allow the devil or anyone else to scribble his dreadful *if* over your faith. Beware of the seeds of unbelief. Satan knows that if he can make us doubt the Father's love or doubt our relationship to God, he will gain a foothold. How can we pray "Our Father in heaven," if we are unsure He is our Father? If we are confident He is our "Abba, Father," we know He understands our weaknesses and needs, forgives our wrongs, protects us in the hour of danger, and will save us in the wilderness. But if we have no Father in Heaven, what shall we do?

Immediately prior to the temptation, the Sonship of Jesus had been confirmed dramatically during His baptism. "And a voice from heaven said, 'This is my Son, whom I love; with him I am well pleased'" (Matt. 3:17). Satan questions the very word of the Father spoken from Heaven. Did Satan actually doubt it? No, the tempter was merely employing one of his favorite strategies of catching a person off guard through their emotions. In this case, Jesus had received the powerful revelation of the Father's love on the banks of the Jordan and is suddenly driven into an intense battle in the wilderness. Such a drastic mood swing from high to low has swept many of us off our feet, but Jesus held steady.

To experience a season of grief or undergo multiple trials in the wilderness is no reason to doubt our sonship. God's Fatherhood does not change with the wind or the heat or the barrenness in the wilderness. Even if you join the prophet Jeremiah and call out to the Lord "from the depths of the pit" (Lam. 3:55), do not listen to the suggestion of the enemy: "If you are a son of God." God is faithful and true, whether you sense His presence and favor or not. Do not doubt Him. Rest your faith upon the promise and the faithfulness of God, not the pleasures of His blessings.

Jesus did not need to nor try to prove that He was the Son of God in the wilderness. He needed to merely continue to live and act in a manner true to who He was. The same is true for us. We are as much a son or daughter when we walk in the scorching heat of the wilderness as when we rejoice on the banks of the Jordan in the light of God's smile.

> Moments will be sprung upon you without warning, in which you will feel that years hang on the issue of an instant. Great tasks will be clashed down before you unexpectedly, which will demand the gathering together of all your power. And there is only one way to be ready for such times as these, and that is to live waiting on the Lord, near Christ, with Him in your hearts, and then nothing will come that is too big for you. However rough the road, and however severe the struggle, and however swift the pace, you will be able to keep it up. Though it may be with panting muscles, yet if you wait on the Lord you will run and not be weary. You will be masters of the crises.
>
> —Alexander Maclaren[1]

ENDNOTE

1. Alexander Maclaren, *The Unchanging Christ and Other Sermons* (London: Alexander & Shepheard, 1889), 21-22.

16

THE POWER OF GOD'S WORD

Every truth about suffering can be twisted into a weapon for or against God. Most often suffering speeds us in the direction we are already heading—whether toward or away from God.

—David McKenna

We are given the details of three temptations of Christ in the wilderness, and within each temptation the devil quotes Scripture. Jesus countered the devil's consistent misuse of Scripture with His own "It is also written" (Matt. 4:7), and His response is one that can aid us immeasurably in the wilderness.

First, notice that Jesus answered all of Satan's lies and doubts with written answers from the Word of God. It is not a matter of discovering secret wisdom or obscure truth. In His conflict with the devil, Jesus went directly to the revealed truth He had gathered through years of studying the Old Testament parchment rolls in Nazareth. He easily discerned that the devil was twisting isolated texts into expressions that were not true to the whole Bible. Jesus shows us that in the wilderness we need to know our Bible well. We need the sustaining word of Christ to dwell in us richly (see Col. 3:16).

Jesus' answers were not only written, but they are simple. Profound answers are always simple, because they come as the result of divine wisdom. Simple does not mean shallow or superficial, but straightforward and uncomplicated. Let "It is written" be your simple answer to whatever you face in the wilderness. No matter what you may be feeling, hold to the Word of God alone—it has never failed.

His answers were also spoken with authority. They are not quoted as assumptions or suggestions.

God knows exactly what we have to endure in the wilderness, and He has written down the exact answers for us. If we try to cook up our own answers, we will find ourselves on the losing side of the battle. But if we accumulate God's answers and use them with authority in the wilderness, the enemy will leave us.

In all His answers, Jesus Christ never said anything that we are not entitled to say. But we must equip ourselves with the written Word, keep our responses simple, and believe and speak them with authority. If we respond as Jesus did, we will clear a path through the wilderness.

Always have "It is written" ready by your side. You must fight if you are to enter heaven. Look to your weapon; it cannot bend or grow blunt; wield it boldly and plunge it into the heart of your enemy. "It is written" will cut through soul and spirit and wound the old dragon himself.

I commend to you the hiding of God's Word in your heart, the pondering of it in your minds. Be rooted and grounded in its teaching and saturated in its spirit.

To me it is an intense joy to search diligently in my Father's book of grace that grows upon me daily. The Bible was written by inspiration in old times, but I have found that not only was it inspired when written, but it is so still. It is not a mere historic document. It is a letter fresh from the pen of God to me. It is not a flower dried and put in a vase, with its beauty clouded and its perfume evaporated. It is a fresh blooming flower in God's garden, as fragrant and as fair as when God planted it.

—Charles Spurgeon[1]

ENDNOTE

1. Charles Spurgeon, *Spiritual Warfare in a Believer's Life* (Lynnwood, WA: Emerald Books, 1993), 75-76.

17

NEVER MISTRUST
THE FATHER

"After fasting forty days and forty nights, he was hungry. The tempter came to him and said, 'If you are the Son of God, tell these stones to become bread.' Jesus answered, 'It is written: "Man does not live on bread alone, but on every word that comes from the mouth of God"'" (Matthew 4:2-4).

The enemy of our soul is cunning and crafty. The devil and his co-workers subtly choose the form of temptation to suit us and quickly change the mode as necessary. He will exploit our weaknesses as long as we allow him to do so. Temptation is always standing and waiting at our door, watching patiently for the slightest opening on our part.

In the wilderness, Jesus bolted the door shut to the enemy, and so may we.

First, Satan appeals to the *neediest* point of the moment. He says, "My goodness, You haven't eaten for forty days. You're starving, but that's no problem. You're the Son of God, and You have the power, so use it." The devil is happy to make suggestions on how we can get what we want or need most on our own. After all, what harm could there be in turning stones to bread at such a needy time? In Jesus' situation, the devil elevates the physical need to break down the moral purpose.

But it is wrong to do anything, even what appears to be a harmless act, at the devil's suggestion. The essence of sin is in the improper use of a proper thing. The only safe thing is to do God's will, to continue to walk according to the Spirit's leading.

The path to victory in the wilderness begins when we recognize what is happening. The devil's lie is that life can be sustained only in one way. We are tricked into believing that we can't live without something. As if we make enough bread, what more can we want? The answer is that God had sustained Christ for forty days without food and could as long as He willed it.

In effect what Jesus is saying is, "My Father knows My every need. My hunger hasn't caught Him unaware. No amount of bread will keep a man alive without a word or an order from God's mouth. If need be, it is better to starve to death than live by sin. I will not mistrust the Father or do anything apart from His leading." Jesus would not take an action or use His power unless it was approved by the Father, which gave Him great strength. Strength increases when we use it properly or refuse to use it improperly.

Jesus' simple reply touches our heart at its neediest point. The unshakable characteristic of Jesus' life was that He trusted His Father all the way to the grave. He trusted His Father for what should be done as well as the way it should be done. For any of us who are under stress of temptation or in the wilderness experience, He has given us the colossal strength to say, "Jesus, who was truly a man, was here, and as a man, He trusted His Father and won. He is at my side.

I will trust in Him and resist and win in the strength of His winning."

In the wilderness, there are two ways you can go. You can go on your own, using your own wits and human strength, or you can turn the situation over to God, who invites you with these words: "Come to me, all you who are weary and burdened, and I will give you rest" (Matt. 11:28). The way to peace of mind and heart is found through surrendering your life to God. You don't have to tell Him how to handle your situation. When you leave your desires in His hands, you can stop fretting because you know that He knows what's best for you. God is waiting for you with open arms.

No one can promise you what God will do in your wilderness. We cannot promise you that your circumstances will change the way you hope. But we can promise that God is perfect in His decisions, timing, and, yes, even in His refusals. And we can promise that God will change *you* in your circumstances, if you allow Him. We can promise you that He will do what's best in your case. His promise stands throughout all time:

"Call upon me in the day of trouble; I will deliver you" (Ps. 50:15).

> The devil is a better theologian than any of us and is a devil still.
>
> —A.W. Tozer

18

NEVER PUT YOUR
FAITH TO THE TEST

*"Then the devil took him to the holy city
and had him stand on the highest point of
the temple. 'If you are the Son of God,' he
said, 'throw yourself down. For it is written: "He will command his angels concern-
ing you, and they will lift you up in their
hands, so that you will not strike your foot
against a stone."' Jesus answered him, 'It is
also written: "Do not put the Lord your
God to the test"'"* (Matthew 4:5-7).

In the second temptation, Satan shifts the
scene dramatically, which is a favorite device of
his. We win a victory over temptation, but a quick
change of surroundings finds us unprepared for a

new temptation, and down we go. The devil moves from enticing Jesus to distrust God by not waiting for bread from God to demonstrating a daring trust in God by testing a promise of God to the limit and to do so immediately.

Satan shrewdly chooses the spot for every temptation. He always waits for a situation and a moment that serves his purpose. He took Christ to the holy city and set Him on the pinnacle of the temple, surrounding Him with a great exhibition of all the outward trappings of religion in order to deceive Him into taking His focus off His inner loyalty to God. Jerusalem, and especially the temple, were where Jesus had probably first experienced a full sense of His Messianic calling and all the spiritual emotions that accompanied that (see Luke 2:41-50). Here everything spoke to Him of His Father.

Jesus had declared that He trusted the Father without reservation. "So you trust in God," Satan implies. "Here's a chance to prove it and allow others to see that beautiful spirit of trust. After all, the angels will bear you up." The tempter plays his cards as a veteran schemer, pulling out a Scripture, editing it cunningly, and repeating it sincerely and convincingly. He was forcing meanings into God's Word that the Holy Spirit never intended and attempting to take the sword of the Spirit from Jesus' hand.

That the angels are ministering spirits and bear us up on their hands is wonderfully true as long as we are living in the context of the entire Psalm 91. The tempter carefully avoids mentioning that we must be living in "the shelter of the Most High" (v. 1). And the devil fails to add the psalmist's allusions to treading and trampling upon the cobra and the serpent (v. 13), which directly follow the quoted section. He knew the Bible well and avoids any mention of himself. He will find a Scripture to prove any of his lies.

Satan's maxim is: "Presume upon God, test His strength, and bring Him the opportunity to show what He means by His promises. After all, if You are the Son of God, a legion of angels will be there for You."

Jesus rebukes this out-of-context quotation with a quotation that clarifies the whole meaning of the passage and reflects a true Son who knows precisely what His Father said and meant. You shall not *test* God to see if He will do as He promises. In the context of Psalm 91, the Israelites had been testing, criticizing, and questioning God. Jesus says that love never tests, because it trusts. Love does not doubt, because it knows. Love requires no test, for it trusts only in God, not tests.

The wilderness is no place to put God to the test, despite the temptation to do so. Never put yourself or allow yourself to be put in a position to try God's promises and put your faith to the test. Remember, to test God always starts with a question, a doubt, a misgiving about God. As a child of God, love for the Father will never push Him to a test, for any reason. What may sound like trust in this case is merely a false trust.

Love simply trusts.

Promises, though they be for a time seemingly delayed, cannot be finally frustrated....the heart of God is not turned though His face be hid; and prayers are not flung back, though they be not instantly answered.

—Timothy Cruso

19

TRUE WORSHIP BELONGS TO GOD ALONE

"Again, the devil took him to a very high mountain and showed him all the kingdoms of the world and their splendor. 'All this I will give you,' he said, 'if you will bow down and worship me.' Jesus said to him, 'Away from me, Satan! For it is written: "Worship the Lord your God, and serve him only."' Then the devil left him, and angels came and attended him" (Matthew 4:8-11).

Another swift shift of scenes. In a moment of time, Satan shows Jesus all the kingdoms and all the glory of all the earth. Martin Luther rightly observed that he who in the first temptation showed himself as a black devil, and in the second as a light, white devil, using even God's own Word, now displays himself as a divine, majestic devil, who comes right out as though he were God himself. The tempter drops his masks and appears as the prince and ruler of this world. In doing so, he exposes the real thing he is after: he would be a god and have Jesus serve him.

The third temptation is the subtlest of temptations. The ruling of the world as God's King was ingrained in Jesus through the consciousness of His mission and advanced by His study of the Hebrew Scriptures. Satan's appeal in effect is this: "I am the prince of this world, and all you see belongs to me. I have power to give the kingdoms to whom I will, and I offer them to you. Let's pull together on this matter of world dominion and do it now. Acknowledge me as Your sovereign, and it's Yours."

This temptation involves a contest of the visible and the invisible. Satan was acknowledged as the "prince of this world" (John 14:30), although his other points were false. It must have been tempting for Jesus to think that He might, at that very moment, grab the reins of all history and take His position of power as ruler and conqueror. Surely He saw radiant visions of the Messiah setting the prisoners free, breaking the bonds of oppression, and bringing healing to the nations. And Satan's offer meant Jesus could avoid the long painful road to Calvary.

The temptation was to get Jesus to take immediate action on what clearly was the eventual will of God. However, nothing but the full obedience of the Son, the obedience unto the death, the absolute doing of the will of God could redeem the prisoner, the widow, and the orphan. We could not be set free apart from Jesus, a true man, giving His life for our sin and becoming our life. Man would be truly free and the grand will of God would be done, but at a phenomenal cost.

Jesus' answer is the commanding word of a conqueror, the King of kings. "Away from me, Satan!" and the tempter slithers away. There is only one sovereign God, Jesus says. The Kingdom of God is only established through a full obedience to Him. There would be no compromise or shortcut for Jesus. Satan is ordered away because he has been utterly vanquished, and the long ordeal of temptation is ended.

Jesus rejects the devil's lie but adds that we shall worship God, giving Him our heart's full adoration. True worship belongs to God alone. We will never be kept upright in the wilderness by merely clinging to "right" theological positions or by hiding behind a formulated faith. We are secure and right only when our prayers and worship are in fellowship with the Father. In the wilderness, an intellectual knowledge of God will never last— only what is genuine abides there.

Faith involves far more than a contemplative folding of the hands and gazing up into the heavens. "The sacrifices of God are a broken spirit; a broken and contrite heart, O God you will not despise" (Ps. 51:17). Faith requires a wholehearted dedication and devotion to God alone, and the wilderness will refine our love for God. Do we wait for and trust in Him? Do we believe the words He has spoken? Do we know Him in the depths of our heart?

There is an end to the wilderness if we will but quietly hold on. When the devil has used up all his devices and has been resisted, he leaves weakened. Temptation resisted strengthens us to higher resistance, but we should know that the enemy will return at "an opportune time" (Luke 4:13). In Jesus, though, we are victors.

> If the devil could be persuaded to write a bible, he would title it "You Only Live Once."
>
> —Sydney Harris

20

STREAMS
IN THE WILDERNESS

*"Then will the eyes of the blind be opened,
and the ears of the deaf unstopped. Then
will the lame leap like a deer, and the mute
tongue shout for joy. Waters will gush
forth in the wilderness and streams in the
desert. The burning sand will become a
pool, the thirsty ground bubbling springs"*
(Isaiah 35:5-7).

The prophet Isaiah was an elderly man when
he wrote these words, yet he opens his old eyes
and sees a panorama of glory in the wilderness. It
is as though he turns his ear and says, "How can
this be? I hear the sound of music and dancing
in the wilderness?" Despite having pronounced

chapter after chapter of woes and visions of divine judgment, Isaiah sees the glory of the Lord and the splendor of God coming to the "desert and the parched land...; the wilderness will rejoice and blossom" (Isa. 35:1). His is a call to a celebration of all that God is about to do.

These remarkable words of the prophet Isaiah record precisely what happened wherever Jesus Christ went (see Matt. 11:5). Blind eyes were opened and saw their God. Deaf ears were unstopped and heard the voice of God. The lame jumped to their feet and leapt and praised God (see Acts 3:7-8), and those who had never spoken suddenly broke a lifetime of silence with songs of praise.

Does the grace of God ever come into the human heart without opening eyes and unstopping ears so that we hear the music of the Good News in Christ Jesus? It is the glory of God that it makes us new creatures in Christ Jesus and continues to shape our lives into His image. Only God could undertake and accomplish such a grand transformation. "Therefore, if anyone is in Christ, he is a new creation: The old has gone, the new has come!" (2 Cor. 5:17). Grace will come to us in the wilderness.

We must understand Isaiah's words about streams coming to the desert. The desert wilderness was famous for its mirages, where the optical illusion of water fools the weary traveler into believing he sees streams and the promise of satisfying his thirst. In the reign of Jesus Christ, there are no delusions of water that never make it to our lips. The dry barren land shall become a pool of refreshing water and abound with bubbling springs and gushing fountains.

The Lord will lead us to streams in the wilderness. The love of Christ will be as spring water to our soul even when the ground is cracking dry and the sand is burning. Whatever our trial or emptiness or loss, we will taste and see that the Lord is good. Delivering grace will be poured into our heart; we shall sing of the mercy and goodness of the Lord in the wilderness. He can turn our wilderness into a lush watered place and give us streams right where we are. He doesn't need to move us out of our circumstances to make us flourish!

My (Ron) friend, Joni Eareckson Tada, is perhaps the most obvious example of how this can happen. A diving accident in 1967 left Joni a quadriplegic in a wheelchair, unable to use her hands. Joni would be the first to tell you that it has not been an easy wilderness. The depression, anxiety, and day-to-day help she needs just to have something close to a normal life for the past forty-five years is not something she would have chosen in a million years. Nevertheless, Joni turned her seeming tragedy into an amazing triumph by the grace of God.

During two years of rehabilitation, she spent long months learning how to paint with a brush between her teeth. Her high-detail fine art paintings and prints are sought after and collected. Due to her best-selling books, beginning with her autobiography, *Joni*, as well as having visited thirty-five countries, Joni's first name is recognized around the world. World Wide Pictures' full-length feature film, *Joni*, in which Joni recreated her own life, has been translated into fifteen languages and shown in scores of countries around the world. If you'd like to know more about what her worldwide ministry is doing today, go to www.joniandfriends.org and be amazed.

Here's what we can learn from Joni's experience: we don't get to choose our lot. Nobody asks us to approve what happens to us in the course of this life. Jesus made it clear that we each receive a cross to bear: "Anyone who intends to come with me has to let me lead. You're not in the driver's seat; I am. Don't run from suffering; embrace it. Follow me and I'll show you how. Self-help is no help at all. Self-sacrifice is the way, my way, to saving yourself, your true self. What good would it do to get everything you want and lose you, the real you? What could you ever trade your soul for?" (Mark 8:34-37 TM).

Perhaps you are facing a "Joni" experience, one that is not going to just go away and return your life to what it was before. God heard Joni's prayer in the wilderness and gave her divine strength and help to overcome her disability. God waits to do the same for you. We cannot tell you what God *will* do for you, but we can tell you what He *can* do for you. He can supply your every need through His omnipotent power, just as He does for Joni.

He will custom tailor a plan that is right for your circumstances and one that will be all and more than you ever dreamed.

No matter what the wilderness brings, if we have Christ in our heart, we have life, we have truth, we have joy, we have peace. God is not limited by our circumstances. Everything that our soul requires, we possess in Christ. We who have Christ in our heart have an inner stream fed by underground channels that are unfazed by the fierce heat or extreme cold of the wilderness. Wherever we go, and whatever we face, we carry within us all the essentials of blessedness. We can relax, knowing God has the power to turn any "bad" circumstance into a good place where we find true joy.

Storms make oaks take deeper roots.

—George Herbert

21

GOD WHISPERS
IN THE WILDERNESS

"The Lord said, 'Go out and stand on the mountain in the presence of the Lord, for the Lord is about to pass by.' Then a great and powerful wind tore the mountains apart and shattered the rocks before the Lord, but the Lord was not the wind. After the wind there was an earthquake, but the Lord was not in the earthquake. After the earthquake came a fire, but the Lord was not in the fire. And after the fire came a gentle whisper. When Elijah heard it, he pulled his cloak over his face and went out and stood at the mouth of the cave" (1 Kings 19:11-13).

Overwhelmed with a sense of failure after fleeing the threats of Queen Jezebel, the prophet Elijah fell asleep in the wilderness, praying that he might die (see 1 Kings 19:4). That's where we left him in our story, but that is not where God left him. Failure is never final when we trust God. The grace of God came as a stream in the wilderness to Elijah in the form of the angel of the Lord, who met Elijah's need for sustenance and strength. Not only was his spirit renewed, but Elijah was led across the desert to the sacred mountain where Moses had personally met with God. There the roar of a great and powerful wind tore the mountain apart, an earthquake shook the mountains with heaves and shudders, and a fire and the billow of smoke filled the forest of scrub oak. All of nature expressed what Elijah had experienced in his soul.

However, the Lord was not in the forces of nature, but in "a gentle whisper," the faintest whisper of a sound (see 1 Kings 19:12). Elijah had to listen intently to hear its calming, quieting, soothing expression, and hearing it, he heard what God had to say. In a world of noise and conflict and confusion, the body and the mind can become fatigued and exhausted, with damaging doubts and fears and anguish invading the heart. In the wilderness, God whispers and brings the healing and fortitude we need.

Best of all, Elijah hears God's voice and is told to "Go back the way you came" (1 Kings 19:15). His lifework of starting a great prophetic movement in Israel was far from over, and God was not finished with King Ahab and Queen Jezebel. Elijah was ready for the next assignment God had for him.

God knows the faithful heart even as we lie down on the wilderness sand and think we can't go on. In the wilderness are streams of living water and angels who know our names. David learned the lesson of the wilderness and tells us: "Be still, and know that I am God" (Ps. 46:10). By God's grace, may we learn it as well.

I have loved to hear my Lord spoken of, and wherever I have seen the print of His shoe in the earth, there have I coveted to put mine also.

—John Bunyan

A WILDERNESS
DEVOTIONAL

Day 1

Lord,

You know everything that's going on in my life. Experts tell us that anxiety is the number one disease in America, and it's true in my life. The panic and anxiety and doubts I feel are hellish to live with, and they are eating me alive.

Despite the wilderness I am in, I declare that there is no night so dark that the morning won't come. Even if things don't turn out the way I hope they will, I believe You hear and see my situation and, if I come to You, can bring me a song in the wilderness.

Regardless of how I feel or what I am frightened of today, I pray this prayer in faith, according to Your Word. I believe that You are keenly aware of my needs and even my desires, and that You have not forgotten me. Help me through this day...and night. Together, we will tackle tomorrow when it comes.

"I will not be anxious about anything, but by prayer and asking, with thanksgiving, I present my requests to you, O God. And I ask for the peace of God that transcends all my understanding and will guard my heart and mind in Christ Jesus.

In His Name, I pray, Amen."

(Based upon Phil. 4:6-7)

Day 2

Father,

How awesome that sounds! I hope that rings inside my head all day...*Father!*

Romans 8:15 tells us that if we have accepted Jesus as our Lord and Savior, we get the right to call You our "Abba," which is an ancient term for our modern word *Daddy*! As I address You this morning, I want to know in my heart that You are truly my Daddy, the Ultimate Father, with every characteristic that can be attributed to that title.

Here's another day and opportunity for me to see You in action. I don't know what You will accomplish today, in me and my situation, but I'm going to believe what I read in Your Word. I'm told there are some things You cannot do. One of them is to lie. So, based upon Your Word, I boldly say:

"You are my Shepherd. I have everything I need. You are going to make me relax in green pastures and lead me beside quiet

waters. You are going to restore my soul and guide me in paths of righteousness for Your Name's sake.

Now even if I walk through a valley as dark as death, I resolve to fear no evil thing, because You are with me. I am comforted by the instruments you use as a Shepherd to keep me safe and in line.

I am going to feast at the table You prepare before me in the presence of all that is against me. Please anoint my head with oil and make the cup You give me to drink overflow. I am sure that goodness and mercy will overtake me now and in the future, and I will wind up living in Your house, with You, forever.

In Jesus' Name, Amen."

(Based upon Ps. 23)

Day 3

My God,

You are the amazing Creator who made me and gave me the skills and abilities to face all that I am facing. You know how often I want to run away from what I'm facing in the wilderness, but there's no way out of my situation. Only You can change my life and situation. I want to hear Your voice today and follow wherever You lead.

What You are doing may not be as visible to my eyes as I know it is to my heart today. What I see is not as real as what You declare. So I will stand on what You have said to me instead of what I think, feel, or even hear others tell me. While Jesus was here on the earth, He taught us to say a prayer like this:

"Father, Your Name is holy! I ask today that Your kingdom would come to me. Your will be done on earth, but also in my home and my family, too, just the same way Your will is always done in Heaven.

Please give from Your storehouse today the food I need. Help me to thank You when I eat it. Please forgive me for all that I have done wrong, every sin; and, in turn, help me to forgive anyone who has wronged me. Please help me with this hard test I am going through and keep me from other tests. But whatever You choose to do, deliver me and keep me from evil.

In the Name of Jesus Christ, Amen."

(Based upon Luke 11:2-4)

Day 4

Father,

Another day. I don't know what it holds, but You do. This may be the day the wilderness ends for me, or it may be the day You turn it into a garden for me. Either way, I firmly believe, without doubting, that You are going to handle what's in store for me.

You know that I've felt that You have me on "hold" here in the wilderness, but that's not true. The truth is that You are holding me in Your arms, loving and caring for me, despite how I feel. Help me look past my feelings and embrace the truth.

"Today, I am going to trust in You with all of my heart, and I will not trust my own limited understanding of things. I resolve that in all of my ways I am going to point to You and trust You to direct this path of mine.

I will not be wise in my own eyes, but I am going to show You the respect and awe You deserve, and I am going to turn away from all that I know to be wrong. In doing this, You promise that it will bring health to my body and strength to my bones.

In Jesus' Name, Amen."

(Based upon Prov. 3:5-8)

Day 5

Dear Father,

I don't know how things look from Heaven, but I am still waiting eagerly for You to move into and through my life and circumstances. I'm trying to wait, but not finding it as easy as I thought. I recognize that besides You, there's absolutely no one else I can appeal to, nor do I want anyone but You.

There are times when I've asked You where You are in all that I'm going through. I know that You're right here beside me, just as You were before I stepped into this wilderness. You were my God and Savior before, and You never moved when my situation changed. It's just that I don't feel Your presence, and I don't understand what You want to do in my life.

Here's my prayer today, based on Your own Word:

"I believe there is no God apart from You. You are the righteous God and Savior—

there is none but You. The others who claim Your status are all useless liars. So I turn to You to be saved, in every way, for You invited all the earth to come to You to be saved. I believe You are God and affirm there is no other.

In Christ's Name, Amen."

(Based upon Isa. 45:21-22)

Day 6

Heavenly Father,

When Jesus walked this earth, He proved that He came from You by the miracles He did. I hear that He is still doing them today. I need one, Lord. I need You to take my situation and turn it for good rather than my letting the situation twist me into a proverbial pretzel. I need Your deliverance, Your healing, Your changing of the circumstances of my life.

Your Word tells of a time when a woman, who had been sick for twelve years and gone to many doctors and spent everything she had with no results, waited for Jesus to pass by her. When He did, she knelt down and broke through the crowd so she could touch the hem of His garment, *knowing* she would be healed. And it happened just as she believed it would.

Based on that passage, my prayer today is:

"Lord, what You did for that woman is what I am asking for me today. I can reach Your garment only by faith, and faith alone. Heal me according to Your great power and impeccable timing.

In Jesus' Name, Amen."

(Taken from Luke 8:43)

Day 7

Father,

C.S. Lewis wondered why You don't use "violins and laughter" to help us grow in character. He answered his own question by recognizing that "pain is Your megaphone to a deaf world."[1] I thank You for using this situation in the wilderness to get my attention and to develop my character. I know that You care more about my character than about my circumstances, and that You are preparing me to live with You forever in Heaven.

You said repeatedly in Scripture, "Never will I leave you; never will I forsake you." This is an anchor for my soul in this wilderness. If You are with me, who can be against me? I *rest* in You, *wait* on You, *hope* in You, and *seek* You. You will sustain me through any challenge and difficulty. You are love; Christ died for me; the Bible is Your living Word; in the cross there is a pardon for me; You are able to keep me from falling.

"Today, I will not fear, for You have redeemed me. You have called me by name; I am yours. When I pass through the waters, You will be with me; and when I pass through the rivers, they will not sweep over me. When I walk through the fire, I will not be burned; the flames will not set me ablaze. Because You have loved me with an everlasting love, You will bring me through the wilderness to the place You have prepared for me. I rest in Your love."

(Based upon Isa. 43:1-2; Jer. 31:3)

Endnote

1. C.S. Lewis, *The Problem of Pain* (New York: HarperCollins, 1940, 1996), 91.

KNOWING
JESUS CHRIST

Perhaps as you've been reading this book, you've discovered that the reason the wilderness makes no sense to you is because you've never had a personal relationship with God. If you're not walking with God, you'll never understand His will for your life in the wilderness. But you can change that.

For over two millennium, one fact has stood fast: Jesus Christ, the only Son of God is the only one who did what He promised to do as proof of His claim as Savior of the world. No other teacher, no other man, ever did the miracles Jesus did, taught the things He taught, died on the cross for our sins, and proved it was all true by rising from the dead. Even historians will admit the truth of this, even if they choose not to follow Him.

What separates us from God and peace with God is sin. If we are honest with ourselves, we cannot deny that from the moment of our birth we have done wrong things—things that make us guilty before God and deserving of His judgment. The Bible calls these wrong things "sin," and sin separates us from God. "For all have sinned and fall short of the glory of God" (Rom. 3:23). And because we are separated from God, we face the awful prospect of "God's wrath" (John 3:36), which is eternal.

Jesus made the ultimate statement by saying, "I am the way and the truth and the life. No one comes to the Father except through me" (John 14:6). He did not say that He simply knew the way to Heaven; Jesus said He is the only way to Heaven. No human effort can give us eternal life. Christ, and Christ alone, is the one and only Savior and Redeemer.

If you have never received Jesus Christ into your life as Lord and Savior, today is your day, and this is your moment to deal with whether you accept His offer. He has done all that is necessary for you to become His child. In order to complete that desire, all that is necessary is a prayer.

> *"Lord Jesus, I believe You are the Son of God, and You died for my sins. I ask You to forgive me of my sin, and I choose to turn from my sins and follow You from this moment on. I invite You to come into my heart and give me eternal life in Your Spirit. Help me to live in a way that pleases and honors You. Amen."*

A FINAL WORD
ABOUT THE WILDERNESS

When the wilderness hits, shock usually is the first response. We may be so taken by surprise that the mind almost shuts out the reality and substitutes just about anything else so we don't have to face facts. It's the only way we can cope with whatever news we just got. Then we hope that we heard wrong, and that everything will be fine.

When it turns out that our situation is as we feared, the next stage is denial. "Perhaps the test was wrong. We'll get a second opinion." "Is it possible you have the wrong person? It can't be my child." But sadly, sometimes the nightmare is reality, and you really are awake, with no hope of returning to the way things were.

What next? Usually, deep grief. The kind of heartbreaking, not to be believed, sorrow. The mother who loses a child descends into another dimension of emotion. The husband who watches his wife run into the arms of another man is inconsolable. The child who grieves over parents who found splitting up easier than staying together is scarred with a lack of security. A thousand different stories, but all have the same numbing hurt.

Because grief cannot be really and truly shared, most of us grieve alone. While many people can be hurt by the same situation, each person has to deal with grief in his or her own private way. No one can take your grief for you, and you cannot take their grief. The only exception is allowing God to do something only He can do, which is to take us in His arms and comfort us with a comfort that is beyond the realm of man. The prophet Isaiah heard God say this: "He has sent me [Jesus] to bind up the brokenhearted,...to comfort all who mourn,... to bestow on them a crown of beauty instead of ashes, the oil of gladness instead of mourning, and a garment of praise instead of a spirit of despair" (Isa. 61:1-3).

After all the stages above, the final one seems to be the acceptance stage. It's the stage when it comes time to put away the earthly methods of hanging on to what will never be again and store them away in a memory box. The old adage that "life goes on" is surely true. As much as we want to scream out to the world, in the final analysis, nobody but God can do anything about it, so we leave it in His hands along with our tears.

When you are deeply hurt and confused, it is not always possible or realistic to be "optimistic" and "positive." Does that mean that God is rendered impotent as a result of your mood? Absolutely not! When we are wounded to the point of helplessness, understanding the promises of God will help change your state of mind.

During this time, don't neglect the things that God has put around you to help you through. Take a walk in the sunshine. Exercise and get some of those endorphins working for you. It's amazing how a short or long walk can alter your perspective! Read God's Word and soak in those amazing words of comfort and promises that He directs specifically to you. Read some good books that strengthen your faith and courage.

Take note that what you are eating may be actually lowering your ability to cope. Too much sugar and caffeine and "junk food" is damaging you, even if it tastes good at the moment. Eating quality foods regularly will ultimately strengthen you for the fight. Get the sleep you need. You'd be surprised by how many problems can be solved by a good night's sleep. If you have friends or family who can take some time to relieve you from your times of stress, don't be too proud to ask.

Do the practical things that you can do for yourself to improve your situation. When worry and stress have sucked you dry of physical strength, your emotional perspective suffers and things look darker than they probably are. That in turn affects your spiritual outlook, and round and round it goes. Get smart about using every thing at your disposal. Some things only God can do, and rest assured, He will, if you trust Him. But He expects you to do what you know you can do with the resources He already has given you.

A Final Word About the Wilderness

In order to be and stay spiritually healthy, God has put a whole host of resources that you need to take advantage of—good churches, Bible study, Christian friends, healthy music, and a steady diet of prayer with God. Remember: praying is more about listening to God than talking at God. He translates our clumsy words into a conversation that delights both Him and us.

It may be that your situation involves issues that require medical or psychological care. For instance, depression should never be viewed lightly. In the case of serious depression, where the person is unable to cope with the ordinary, routine duties of life, a medical checkup is advisable. Some forms of depression or other states of mind are chemically based and are greatly helped by proper medication.

Most importantly, through it all, remember that only God lasts forever. Both the good and bad times will fade away. Before you know it, you will be either standing in the light of His deliverance or in the light of His presence. Either way, problem solved!

In the meantime, the famous prayer of Reinhold Niebuhr is appropriate,

> God grant me the serenity to accept the things I cannot change, the courage to change the things I can, and the wisdom to know the difference.

OTHER BOOKS BY
LANCE WUBBELS

If Only I Knew

Dance While You Can

I Wish for You

Each Day a New Beginning

The Lord Is My Shepherd

A Time for Prayer

To a Child Love is Spelled T-I-M-E

In His Presence

Jesus: The Ultimate Gift

One Small Miracle

ABOUT THE AUTHORS

Ron DiCianni

Ron DiCianni is a Christian cleverly disguised as an author and artist. For more than two decades he has been passionate to use the creative arts to indelibly impact this generation. Using words, paint or voice, Ron has one message: Jesus! You can view his efforts at www.TapestryProductions.com and contact him there at (877) 827-7763.

Lance Wubbels

Lance Wubbels is the vice president of literary development at Koechel Peterson & Associates and Shiloh Road Publishing. He has authored several fiction and nonfiction books, including five best-selling Hallmark Gift Books and three gift books with Inspired Faith. He has won two Gold Medallion book awards from the Evangelical Christian Publishers Association.

A LAST WORD FROM
RON DICIANNI

May I end with a personal benediction meant just for you? As you might imagine, it's from God's Word....Again, I'm just the messenger here! Maybe this entire book came into your hands just to hear this from God Himself:

> *"Now may the God of peace, who through the blood of the eternal covenant brought back from the dead our Lord Jesus, that great Shepherd of the sheep, equip you with everything good for doing his will, and may he work in us what is pleasing to him, through Jesus Christ, to whom be glory for ever and ever. Amen"* (Hebrews 13:20-21).

OTHER BOOKS BY RON DiCIANNI

Tell Me the Secrets

Tell Me the Story

Safely Home

Holding Heaven

Tell Me the Promises

Tell Me About Heaven

Were You There

Beyond Words

Sacred Art

OTHER BOOKS BY
LANCE WUBBELS

If Only I Knew

Dance While You Can

I Wish for You

Each Day a New Beginning

The Lord Is My Shepherd

A Time for Prayer

To a Child Love is Spelled T-I-M-E

In His Presence

Jesus: The Ultimate Gift

One Small Miracle

ABOUT THE AUTHORS

Ron DiCianni

Ron DiCianni is a Christian cleverly disguised as an author and artist. For more than two decades he has been passionate to use the creative arts to indelibly impact this generation. Using words, paint or voice, Ron has one message: Jesus! You can view his efforts at www.TapestryProductions.com and contact him there at (877) 827-7763.

Lance Wubbels

Lance Wubbels is the vice president of literary development at Koechel Peterson & Associates and Shiloh Road Publishing. He has authored several fiction and nonfiction books, including five best-selling Hallmark Gift Books and three gift books with Inspired Faith. He has won two Gold Medallion book awards from the Evangelical Christian Publishers Association.